SPELL IT RIGHT!

Heron Books, Inc.
20950 SW Rock Creek Road
Sheridan, OR 97378
USA

heronbooks.com

Fourth Edition © 1997, 2020 Heron Books

ISBN: 978-0-89-739234-1

Printed in the USA

1 July 2020

CONTENTS

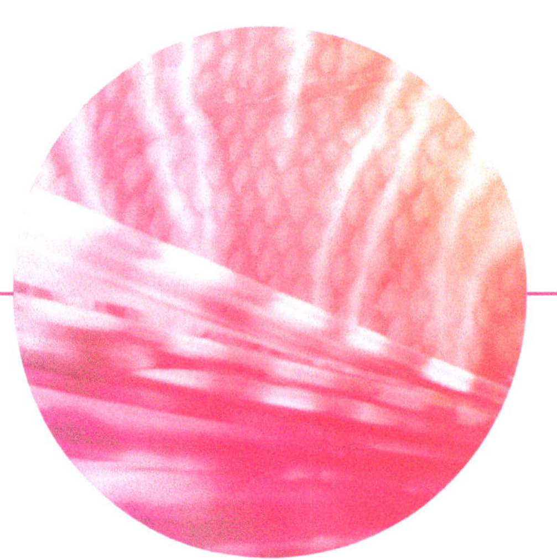

WHAT IS DISCIPLINE?

1

What Is Discipline?

Discipline is being able to do something in a way that might not be easy but it works, and then doing it that same way each time.

Have you ever tried to do something the easy way, but it ended up not working well?

Let's look at a simple example of packing for a trip. You could wait until the last minute, pull out your suitcase and throw in clothes along with a few other things. This is easy to do and doesn't take long. But when you arrive where you're going, you notice your clothes are wrinkled, and you've forgotten not only your toothbrush, but also your bathing suit. So you can't brush your teeth or go swimming!

Or you might think ahead about where you're going, make a short list of the things you know you'll need, get them together, fold your clothes, and put everything neatly into your suitcase. It takes more discipline to pack like this. But when you arrive, your clothes look nice, and you have everything you need. Packing wasn't as quick or easy as the first way. It took a little more time and thought. But it sure worked a lot better.

Sometimes people think discipline is a bad thing. Some people even use the word "discipline" when they mean "punishment." But discipline, doing something in a way that works, and then doing it that way every time, can actually be a very good thing.

PROFESSIONALS

Professionals are experts at what they do, and they use discipline all the time. It's how they become professionals.

Let's take the example of a professional soccer player. She's an expert at dribbling, passing and shooting the ball. She doesn't just happen to be good at these, she used discipline to learn them.

First she learned how to handle the ball in simple ways that worked and practiced over and over until she was very good. After that she gradually learned more difficult moves and tricks and practiced and practiced these until she was expert at them.

The soccer player who never really bothers to practice the best ways of handling a ball never gets very good at soccer. Maybe she just wants to learn the tricks. But she's never had enough discipline to become expert enough at the basic skills needed to learn the tricks. So she'll never even be good at those.

If you think of someone who is very good at something and you look closely, you'll see that they've learned the best ways to do things, even if they're hard, and then practiced them over and over. They've used discipline to become very good at what they do.

If you think of someone who is not good at things, you will probably see a person who doesn't use discipline. You'll see someone who doesn't bother to learn and practice.

So now you know a little about discipline. It's a big part of how people get really good at things. Using discipline, you can get very good at just about anything you'd like to be able to do.

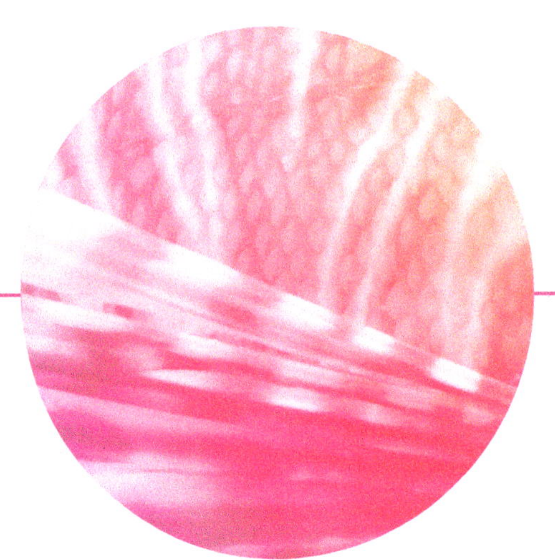

THE PARTS OF DISCIPLINE

2

The Parts of Discipline

Now that we have an idea of what it is, let's take a look at a few different parts of discipline.

USING SELF-CONTROL

Self-control is getting yourself to do something or act some way you know is right, even if it's not easy.

Imagine your room is a mess, and you're tired of not being able to find things. The answer is, of course, to clean the room up, but what's fun about that? You'd much rather go out and do something with your friends. Still, you can't find your favorite sweatshirt or the ten dollars you earned the day before.

So you get yourself to go in and start picking things up and putting them where they belong. You throw stuff away and take out the trash. You put your dirty clothes in the laundry hamper. You pull out everything underneath your bed and put it away. Then you make the bed.

Pretty soon you've found your sweatshirt, the ten dollars and the book you were in the middle of last week that you never finished, and the room is neat enough to see where things are. Even though you wanted to do something else, you got yourself to do the things you knew would give you a neater room. This took self-control.

Self-control is very useful, because with enough self-control you can accomplish things that would otherwise be too hard. Self-control is a big part of discipline. You can't have discipline without it.

DOING EXACT STEPS

Often, when you're learning to do something, you will find that people have worked out a way of doing it that gives a good result. This is often a set of exact steps.

A recipe is a good example. In cooking, a good recipe is often the result of someone making the same dish again and again to find an exact set of steps that make it come out the tastiest. People can then follow these exact steps and the food they make turns out to be delicious.

DOING THINGS THE WAY THAT WORKS BEST

In life, there are certain ways of doing things that people have discovered work the best. In writing, for example, you use sentences, paragraphs, punctuation and good spelling, because this is the best way to write things others can understand.

This can be a lot to remember. You might think it's easier not to do it all. But you'll soon find that it's not easier for your readers because they can't understand what you're trying to say. It just doesn't work!

Just like self-control and following the exact steps for doing things, part of discipline is doing things a certain way that people have found works the best.

PRACTICING

Can you think of something you do very well? Can you think of how you use discipline when you do it? In other words, how do you use self-control, do exact steps, and do things a certain way that works?

And then do you have to practice? This is part of discipline too. Experts use self-control, learn the steps and ways for doing something, and then practice and practice. Eventually they don't have to think about the steps. They can just do them automatically. If you are very good at something, you know how this works.

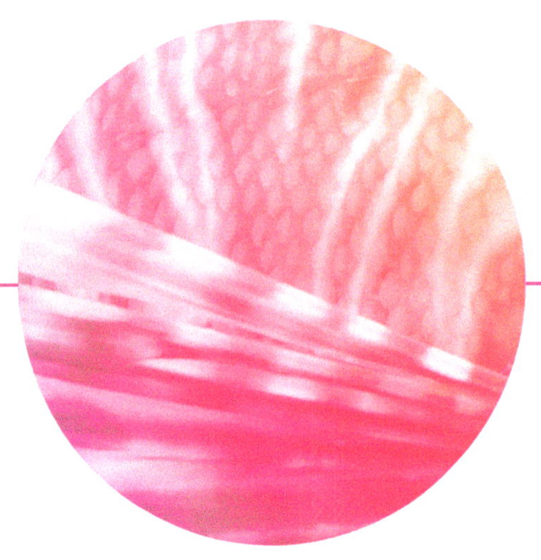

DISCIPLINE HAS REWARDS

3

Discipline Has Rewards

Discipline has big rewards. People who use discipline can become *very good* at things they want to be able to do. If there is something you want to be good at, you might think of how discipline could help you with that.

People who are professionals and experts have used discipline, sometimes for many years, to become very good at what they do.

In fact, they are often the ones who help us by discovering even better ways of doing things. In this way, they help make the world a better place.

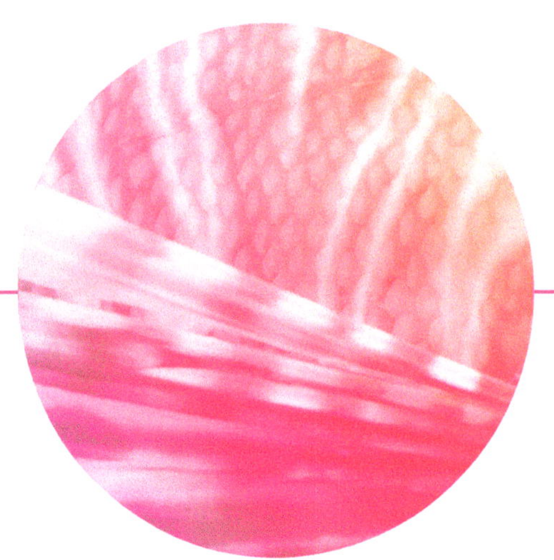

WRITING THAT'S CLEAR AND EASY TO READ

4

Writing That's Clear and Easy to Read

Now that we have some understanding of discipline, let's take a look at what it has to do with writing.

One big way we all share our thoughts and ideas with others is through writing. We write stories, books, essays, poems, texts, e-mails and notes. Even though there is a lot of digital communication in today's world, writing has not become any less important. In fact, it's probably become even more important because now, with the internet, more people can use writing to share their ideas with other people.

To get our ideas across to people we're sharing with, our writing has to be clear and easy to read. How do we make it this way?

One way is punctuation. Punctuation is useful because it signals when written ideas start and stop. Otherwise they all run together and become hard to understand.

Punctuation is also helpful in getting across the *feeling* of what you are saying. For example, when you are excited you can use an exclamation point (!).

Another way is by writing in sentences and paragraphs. Without these, you'd have a long string of words and ideas. It would be hard to tell when one idea or subject was done and another was starting.

Spelling is a third way. This is helpful because a correctly spelled word is easy to recognize and understand. Your readers can be sure that what they are reading is what you meant to say.

Writing that has all these can be read easily and its message clearly received.

Learning each one of these takes some discipline. You have to learn how things are done, practice them, and then do them when you write.

But they are worth learning. Good writers know how to make their writing easy to read and understand. And readers appreciate this.

Something you may not have thought about is that your writing makes an impression on other people. It shows things about you. When we read something written by someone, their handwriting, punctuation and spelling tell us things about them. A person who is actually quite smart and hard working might look lazy or dull because their writing is sloppy and has misspellings.

Writing neatly and clearly with good punctuation and spelling not only makes people think well of you, it is inviting. People enjoy good, clear writing and will *want* to read what you have written!

HOW TO WRITE WITH GOOD SPELLING

5

How to Write with Good Spelling

Now let's take a look at spelling. The question is, what's the best way to create writing with good, clear spelling that's easy for others to read?

One obvious way is simply learning to spell more and more words. For some people this comes sort of naturally. For others it can take some practice. Whichever way is true for you, the more words you know how to spell, the easier and more expressive your writing can be.

Another way is knowing how to do a good job *checking your spelling. This has two parts.*

1. Checking your spelling *while* you write.

   This means that when you're writing and you notice you're not sure how to spell a word, you look it up and get the spelling right.

2. Checking your spelling *after you're done* writing.

   This means when you've finished writing, carefully checking over your spelling, and finding and fixing any mistakes.

In the next two chapters we'll talk more about how to do each of these.

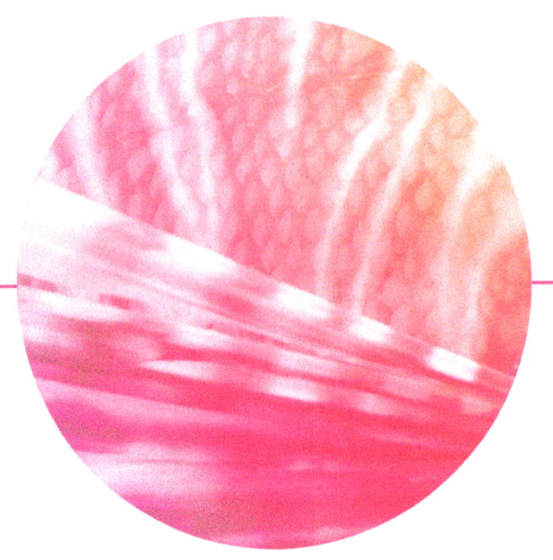

CHECKING SPELLING WHILE YOU WRITE

6

Checking Spelling While You Write

Sometimes you can be writing along and realize you want to use a word you're not sure how to spell. What to do? The simplest thing to do is stop and get the correct spelling.

One way to do this is by checking it in a dictionary. And if you can't find the word you're looking for, you might ask someone to help you. This way you'll *know* the word is spelled right, and you won't have to check it later.

Similarly, sometimes you might be writing along and notice that a word you've written just "doesn't look right." We all know what that's like. When this happens it's time to stop and check to make sure your spelling is correct.

Checking spelling takes discipline. First you have to be willing to notice that you're not sure of a word, or that you don't know how to spell it. Then you have to make yourself stop and look it up to get it right.

This might not seem easy, but it works. Not only will you get the right spelling, but each time you do this your spelling will improve a little. Gradually you'll know more and more words and will be a more confident speller. And as this happens, it will become easier and faster to say what you want.

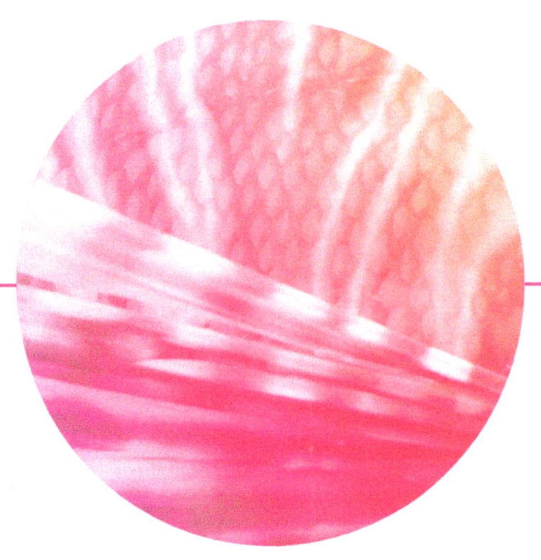

CHECKING SPELLING AFTER YOU WRITE

7

Checking Spelling After You Write

The other part of checking your spelling comes after you've finished a piece of writing. Whether it's a story, an email or a short note, you read over what you've written to make sure it's clear and easy to read. This is called **proofreading**.

When you proofread a piece of writing you carefully read over every sentence and each word to find and fix anything that's not clear. Does each sentence make sense? Have you put punctuation in the right places? Are the words spelled right?

This might seem unnecessary, especially when you've just finished writing something. You might feel sure it has no errors in it. After all, if you had made a mistake you would have fixed it right away!

But even the best writers can get so busy concentrating on what they want to say that they don't always notice misspellings and other little mistakes here and there.

Good proofreading takes discipline. It's not always easy to carefully read every sentence you've written, clean up any mistakes and make sure everything is clear.

But if you do this, it works. You end up with a piece of writing you can be proud of, one that's easy for others to read.

HOW TO PROOFREAD YOUR SPELLING

Here are some possible steps for proofreading your spelling.

1. Read each sentence and look at the spelling of each word.

2. Fix any words you know are wrong.

3. If you come to a word you think *might* be right but you're not sure, check it. This includes words that "just don't look right" to you.

4. Sometimes it's easier to do these steps one paragraph at a time. This way you can make sure each paragraph is correct before going on to the next one.

5. Check over your piece of writing *as many times as needed* to be sure all the spelling is correct.

GOOD PROOFREADING TAKES PRACTICE

At the beginning, careful proofreading may seem like a lot of work. And you may not catch all your spelling errors at first. But if you keep trying and keep working at it, you'll get better and better and eventually you'll get faster too.

SPELLING WITH SUCCESS

8

Spelling with Success

Some people think they have trouble with spelling when it's really just their discipline that needs improving.

If you continue learning new words, continue checking your spelling as you write and continue getting better and better at your proofreading, this will show in your writing!

www.ingramcontent.com/pod-product-compliance
Lightning Source LLC
LaVergne TN
LVHW060330080326
833046LV00030BA/139

* 9 7 8 0 8 9 7 3 9 2 3 4 1 *